MY FIRST EBAY SALE

Start your own e-commerce business from home: A simple, straight forward step-by-step guide to getting started on eBay. Today!

Joseph Henry

My First Publishing

Copyright © 2021 Joseph Henry

Copyright © 2021 Joseph Henry

All rights reserved The characters and events portrayed in this book are fictitious.

Any similarity to real persons, living or dead, is coincidental and not intended by the author.

No part of this book may be reproduced, or stored in a retrieval system, or transmitted in any form or by any means, electronic, mechanical, photocopying, recording, or otherwise, without express written permission of the publisher.

Please note this book is provided as an information resource only, it is no way a demonstration of advice or amplitude.

Before embarking on any course of action please do further research and due diligence to ensure that any course of action is relevant for your situation.

Results from ecommerce may vary.

Dedicated to Cathrine, Meeko, Mousey & Major!

This book has been written for ease of use and reading.
Each chapter is a tiny nuggets of information to help you absorb the information.

Each part of the book covers a part of the eBay selling process.

At the top of the pages are chapter names and page numbers to help you reference actions in the future. Each chapter has white space below to allow you to write notes.

This is after all an action book.

Take action!

Any questions contact me on instagram @homeworkinghenry

JOSEPH HENRY

CONTENTS

Title Page
Copyright
Dedication
Epigraph

Introduction	1
Part One:	4
Why sell on eBay?	5
eBay' Size	6
Advertising & Marketing	7
Ease of use	8
eBay is Old (Or Should we say mature!)	9
Flexibility	10
Software	11
Work-Life Balance	12
Decluttering	13
Selling on eBay is fun	14
Part Two:	15

What you need to get started selling on eBay	16
Email address	18
Bank Account & PayPal account	20
An eBay Account	22
Things To Sell	24
Laptop Or Mobile Phone	26
A Place to Store your Inventory	27
Packaging & Shipping Materials	29
The Last thing you need	31
Part Three:	33
How to find stock to sell on ebay	34
Part Four:	37
How to create an eBay account	38
Naming your eBay account	40
How to create a listings on ebay	41
Golden eBay Rules	42
Be The Customer	43
Be Truthful & Point Out Flaws	45
Fill In Every Box	46
Creating an advert or listing	48
Five Step Listing	49
Part Five:	51
Headline	52
Six rules to writing a good headline	53

Category	55
Condition	56
Item Description Box	57
Selling Details	59
Format	60
Reasons to go with an "auction"	61
Reasons to "Fix Price"	62
Start Date	63
Price	64
VAT	65
Tick Boxes	66
Delivery Details	67
Package Dimensions	68
Item Location	69
Sell it faster	70
eBay Photography School	71
15 steps for Photographs	72
Golden Rules: Photography	74
Get ready to list your first item	75
ParT Six:	77
How to ship your sales	78
The Shipping process	80
Tips for good postage and packing	82
Shipping and Packaging Shopping List	84

Part Seven:	85
How to manage your money on eBay	86
Key Accounting Concepts	88
Revenue/Sales	89
Profit	90
Cashflow	91
Capital Expenditure	93
Drawings	94
Cost of Sales	95
Getting started managing your ebay income	96
Weekly Money Management	98
Next steps	101
Further Reading and Resources	102
Books on Accounting	103
Books on eBay Selling & Online Business	104
Bank Accounts and Payment Gateways	106
Payment Gateways for eBay	107
Bank Accounts	108
Shipping and Packaging Items	109
About The Author	111
Books By This Author	113

INTRODUCTION

Would you like to make some extra money?

We all would, especially if it means we are able to do it from home and on the internet. Making money online seems easy if all the adverts on YouTube, Facebook and the Internet are to be believed.

The adverts are always full of people driving fast cars that are sharing "one quick trick" that will also have you making millions in months, weeks, or even hours!

Sadly, the only people who will make money from these adverts are the people who are selling the course, and generally they have never made a penny on eBay, Amazon or any other platform.

However, we are not selling the "get quick rich" approach to ecommerce, we are going to show you how you can make your first sale on ebay. Of course how much you make on eBay is down to the products you source, the hard work you put in, the time and of course market conditions.

What we will promise you is that if you put in the time, are patient eBay will repay you.

eBay really is the grandfather of the internet and helped bring e-commerce to the masses before the masses they even knew what e-commerce was. eBay might not be as sexy as Amazon, or as funky as Etsy or as hip as Vinted, it is however, still the best place to get started on your own ecommerce journey.

In this ebook we are going to take you from zero to your first sale on ebay and hopefully make your first £99/$99 on eBay.

Now before we begin a word of warning.

- eBay is not a get rich quick scheme - it requires hard work, time, and patience.
- I am no expert, just a fellow traveller on the journey. I might be a few steps ahead, but with diligence you can join me, and I hope overtake me.
- Please do your research and due diligence before embarking on any course of action.
- eBay and eCommerce changes all the time.
- The principles stay the same, the tactics

and steps can sometimes change.
- This book is designed with UK sellers in mind.
- However, international sellers will also find this book useful.

What we are going to cover in this book:

- Why sell on eBay.
- What you need to get started.
- Finding products to sell.
- How to create an account.
- How to create a listing.
- How to ship effectively.
- How to manage the money from sales.

PART ONE:

WHY SELL ON EBAY?

WHY SELL ON EBAY?

In today's modern world, there are so many choices when it comes to selling and starting your ecommerce journey. For instance you can sell on Facebook, eBay, Amazon, Vinted, Poshmark, VarageSale, Gumtree, Shopify, Instagram shops, Magento, BigCommerce to name a few.

That is some range of choice, and to be honest, for the beginner most of these channels just do not make sense. Our suggestion, given the title of the book, is to start with the granddaddy of ecommerce: EBAY!

Now I can hear you say "why eBay?", great question, I am glad you asked. To answer this question we have put together our top 9 reasons why you should get started on eBay.

EBAY' SIZE

eBay has 250 million searches per day, that's 3,000 per second. That's 3,000 people per second looking for items to buy.

This means that you will already have a potential customer base ready to buy your products from day one.

ADVERTISING & MARKETING

eBay is the biggest advertiser on Google pay per click and one of the biggest advertisers across the internet.

This means that as you start selling on eBay you are going to benefit from one of the most sophisticated marketing and advertising teams around.

EASE OF USE

eBay has the easiest entry point for ecommerce on the internet. eBay is easy to use, and it is free to get started.

This means that you are able to get going quickly, take action and not have to worry about having money upfront.

EBAY IS OLD (OR SHOULD WE SAY MATURE!)

e Bay has been around for 25 years. It's unlikely to go anyway anytime soon. eBay is old, and this is a good thing.

The internet is full of start-ups that are here today and gone tomorrow. However, eBay have been around since long before the average Tik Tok user was born.

This means that consumers trust eBay and understand how it works. You are able to benefit from that heritage and trust which has been built up over a quarter of a century from your very first day of trading.

FLEXIBILITY

eBay is a true sandbox that allows you to sell what you like and how you like. With eBay you are able to sell pretty much almost anything, be it designer gear to a gearboxes.

eBay has it all and allows you to have the flexibility in price, shipping, time to dispatch, headline writing and photography. It really is all down to you.

SOFTWARE

There is no software to install or special computer 'know how' needed.

This is brilliant, as platforms like Shopify and Magento can be real pains to get started with.

All eBay needs is a smartphone, an email address and the eBay app to get going.

This means with a few clicks you are ready to rock-and-roll.

WORK-LIFE BALANCE

You can easily schedule eBay selling around your job and home life. eBay lends itself as a platform to fit around your life. Because it offers flexibility in shipping dates or sales methods.

For example, if you can only get to the post office every Friday, change your dispatch time to 7 days and the dispatch and shipping of products can be fitted into that slot. Without breaking any eBay rules or customer expectations.

This means that you can achieve the balance you need from eBay.

DECLUTTERING

eBay allows you to declutter your house and make a few quid as well.

Kaching!!

Decluttering your home can seem a real waste as you start throwing out all the unwanted stuff from your house. However, with eBay it will allow you to sell most things whilst decluttering.

This means you can get that zen like feeling whilst topping up the bank balance and not adding to landfill.

SELLING ON EBAY IS FUN

Selling on ebay is actually good fun. There is a great feeling when you get up in the morning and see a little red dot in the corner of the eBay app and realise that someone has bought one of your products.

This means that not only will you be making some money on eBay, it is good fun as well.

PART TWO:

WHAT YOU NEED TO GET STARTED SELLING ON EBAY

WHAT YOU NEED TO GET STARTED SELLING ON EBAY

Getting started selling on eBay is easy. It can seem intimidating thinking about what to list, how to write a listing, dealing with customers, shipping and returns. Taken all together it does seem like a lot of new skills to acquire.

However, breaking it up into small bite-sized chunks makes learning ebay far easier and way less stressful.

Below is a handy guide to everything that you will need to get started. Phew, I bet you are glad we put this together.

You need the following:

    1. Email address.

2. Bank account and PayPal account.
3. An eBay account.
4. Things to sell.
5. Laptop or mobile phone.
6. Place to store the goods.
7. Packaging material.

Not much at all to start selling on eBay is it?

EMAIL ADDRESS

For almost everything on the internet you need an email address. eBay is no different. You will need an email address to get started.

Now there is a debate whether you should use a new separate email address or your everyday email address when you first start out on your eBay journey.

Personally, when we started out on our eBay journey, we began using our own personal email address and then grew into a more professional email address and set up.

At the start you can just use your own account, as you are just getting started.

However, I would recommend that your email address is fit for purpose, e.g **wilsonsebaystore@gmail.com** rather than **bigboywilson887@hotmail.com** as it is more professional and does separate personal and professional email.

Top three free email address providers are listed below. However, other email providers are available and please check out each one before deciding.

Gmail from Google - **https://gmail.com** - great for Android users.

Outlook by Microsoft - **https://outlook.com** - great for everyone.

iCloud Mail by Apple - **https://icloudmail.com** - great for apple users.

BANK ACCOUNT & PAYPAL ACCOUNT

Why do you need a bank account and a Paypal account? So eBay can pay you all that lovely money from your sales.

eBay requires these as a must. Gone are the days of being able to write cheques for payment. If you remember this you are either a hardcore, early days interneter or very old, like me!

Recently eBay introduced managed payments, a system that cuts out PayPal from its platform. Customers can still pay for items using PayPal, but it's not the only option. We have found that this has made dealing with all the cash from ebay so much easier and frankly cheaper as well.

Get a separate bank account to start your journey with eBay and you will find the entire experience far more satisfying, pleasant and less stressful.

Having a separate bank account will allow you to manage the money you make via ebay and in time to reinvest the profits. Many people when they get started on eBay use their own personal accounts and find that they get money mixed up and do not enjoy their profits or mix up their costs with personal expenses.

There are various "free" digital first banks that are a great starting point in your search for a bank account

Free app accounts & Paypal

Monzo - **https://monzo.com/**

Starling - **https://www.starlingbank.com/**

Tide - **https://www.tide.co/**

Paypal - **https://www.paypal.com/uk**

Of course, before you use any financial product or service, please do your own research and due diligence to ensure that it is suitable for you and your personal circumstances.

AN EBAY ACCOUNT

Now it goes without saying that you will need an eBay account. My suggestion is that you use the account you already shop with on ebay. That is of course if you have used eBay in the past. Amazingly some people have not used eBay.

You might be thinking 'didn't he say earlier keep your business and personal separate'? I know, I know, you are going to be saying 'but shouldn't we be acting professionally and keeping business and pleasure separate?'

With your finances that is certainly very true. However, when it comes to your eBay account, it very much makes sense to use an account you have had for a while for a number of reasons.

Reason 1: it's just easier and quicker to get going. Defeating procrastination is important.

Reason 2: age plays a part in the algorithm that decides what products to show people. Having an older account will help you rank higher.

Reason 3: you will already have feedback. Nothing is worse than an account with no feedback. It will slow down initial sales. However, never fear, everyone does have to start somewhere even if you are new to eBay. It will just slow down those few initial sales.

At this stage, taking that first step is all that matters!

THINGS TO SELL

Once you have your account, your bank account (and PayPal), your eBay account you are now ready to go!

So all you need are things to sell. This is where it gets really, really exciting!

Now you could go and get out into the big wide world and hustle, hustle, hustle and find good fantastic stock to sell.

Or you could just look closer to home.

Everyone has things that they do not need anymore, that someone else might need. You may think it is junk. But your junk is another persons 'must have'.

For instance, old instruction manuals. They could go in the bin or they could go on eBay for someone who repairs VCRs and wants the manuals to go with the finished item. Or old books that you have read, but other people have not read and would like to read.

Used books is one of the biggest markets on the internet. A small unknown company called Amazon started with books.

Other ideas for things to sell on eBay:

- Old clothes, wash them, iron them and list them.
- Pile of clutter in the attic. Get up there and get it sorted, get it listed.
- Garage full of old bikes, toys and other clutter. Get them listed also.

Start at home and declutter the house first to start your selling journey.

If you are decluttering it will go in the bin anyway, so you may as well list it.

There are a whole host of ways to find products to sell on eBay: charity shops, Facebook marketplace, dumpster diving, or just asking friends and family.

However, we suggest that you start small and start at home. Starting at home will give you the confidence to continue selling and it will teach you the ropes without having to spend money.

LAPTOP OR MOBILE PHONE

These are a must if you are going to be selling on ebay. If however, you only have a very basic smartphone that will be enough.

Essentially, you just need to be able to download the eBay app to get started.

If you can connect to the internet with a computer, laptop, tablet or smartphone you will be fine.

Remember, this is about starting this journey today.

A PLACE TO STORE YOUR INVENTORY

This does not need to be anywhere fancy. Just some boxes in a corner that you keep the items separate from everyday life and allow you to easily pick, parcel and ship the items when the time comes.

If you have a garage, a spare bedroom, a dry shed or attic space this is even better.

Essentially you want the items to be away from the rest of your other stuff because it stops them getting broken in between listings and shipping. Keeping the items separate also allows you to ship more quickly and with less hassle and stress.

Remember, the essence of this approach is for it to

be easy and simple.

Start organised. Stay organised.

PACKAGING & SHIPPING MATERIALS

The chances are in your house you have all the materials that you need to be able to ship the items that you sell initially. From old boxes, cuts of bubble wrap, too old newspapers you will be amazed what you can find around the house for free.

Basically search those draws, those cupboards and those boxes, those nooks and those crannies.

Ask friends, ask families, ask neighbors if need be ask your granny.

You want to find as much packaging material for free as possible.

Always keep all the packaging materials that you

find when you get a delivery to your house.

This is a great way at recycling (Brilliant!) and saves money (double brilliant!!).

Visit your local supermarket and ask if they have boxes or other waste materials that you can borrow. Even your corner shop can be a great place to get packaging material.

At the start of this project, not spending money is important. As you want as much of that lovely money as you can keep to reinvest or treat yourself.

THE LAST THING YOU NEED

The last thing you need is hard work and patience. As you can see, this is not much to get started selling on eBay.

But.

It.

Does.

Take.

Time.

At present it might seem like there is alot to take in, and indeed alot to do. However, many of the tasks above will only take a few hours. If that.

If you looking for inspiration check out our eBay shop - **https://www.ebay.co.uk/str/FirecatsUK** - remember we started small, just like you. We are still on our growth journey, but hey, it's all about the journey.

PART THREE:

HOW TO FIND STOCK TO SELL ON EBAY

HOW TO FIND STOCK TO SELL ON EBAY

Many people, even seasoned veterans of the eBay game will tell you that one of the hardest parts of eBay is finding the right products to sell. As you are new to eBay you have one great advantage over the veterans - easy access to products to sell. The unwanted, or indeed items that are inhabiting your home.

Your home is a treasure trove of products that you can sell. Many of us have huge amounts of unwanted, unneeded stuff. Many of us just do not realise that we have as much stuff as we do own, that we just never use again.

Searching your home for items to sell is a great place to start as you find items to sell, declutter the house and bring in some much needed money. These are all excellent thing that can happen when you get started on your ebay journey.

Need some ideas on how and what to declutter and sell. We have put nine great ideas below:

Get all your clothes out and try them all on. Those that don't fit - list it on eBay.

Review your bookshelf - have you read the book? Will you read it again? If you have answered Yes and then No - list it on eBay.

Toys your kids have outgrown - list it on eBay.

If you have an attic, go into the attic. If you have not used it in the last year I suggest that you get it listed on eBay ASAP.

Do you keep old coffee jars? Clean them and list it on eBay.

Do you have old electronics manuals to out of date appliances? List it on eBay.

Do you have old hobbies or hobbies that you have old kit? List it on eBay.

Art work you made. List it on eBay.

Shed or garage - sift through and list anything that you have not used in a year. In all likelihood you are never going to use it again, list it on eBay.

The above ideas give you a great basis for getting started decluttering and listing items on eBay.

One word of warning. Decluttering can get addictive and then lead to a backlog of products that need to be on listed onto eBay.

Big piles of unlisted stock can be demotivating, so we suggest that you focus on one room/source of stock at a time, find all the products, list them all, then move on.

It is a slightly slower process. However, following it you will pace yourself and learn more about what sells and how to sell items as you move from one room to another.

You will enjoy both the financial and mental benefits of this process of decluttering and listing items on eBay.

Your house is a great resource for getting started on ebay! Make it the first step on your ecommerce journey.

PART FOUR:

HOW TO CREATE AN EBAY ACCOUNT

HOW TO CREATE AN EBAY ACCOUNT

Now, it is time to create an eBay account. Now the way to do this depends on whether you are using the app or going via the website.

I will discuss how to set up the account via the app as that is the most easily accessible method to get going. Literally all you need to do is whip your phone out right now and do the following:

Step 1) Download the app from your smartphones app store of choice. Typing eBay into the search bar at the top will suffice to find the app. Hit install or download.

Step 2) Go make a cup of coffee, tea, hot chocolate

or beverage of choice. It should be downloaded once you have your cup of coffee in hand. If not sooner.

Step 3) Open up the eBay app and click on the My eBay section.

Step 4) Click on the section Sign In.

Step 5) At this stage you will be presented with a range of options that will include Signing in with Facebook, Signing In with Google, Signing in with Apple (if on an Apple phone) or username. Ignore these and click on the smaller option at the bottom 'Create an account'.

Step 6) Add in your email address, first name and surname and any other information that is required when you sign up.

Step 7) Click on the blue button to finish.

You now have an ebay account. WooHoo!!

NAMING YOUR EBAY ACCOUNT

Before you go in "balls deep" on your account, make sure to take the time to name the account in a way that will give you longevity. If you set up an account a few years ago and named it Fidget Spinners Superstore it is not a name that will last the test of time.

However, this is ebay so names are not as important as you may think. They are useful as you grow bigger and become more established.

What we suggest is your store name should be something that is a "brand" but is simple to remember. Calling your store Bella's Boutique or Coreens Closet or David's Deals is not a bad move.

Just keep it simple.

HOW TO CREATE A LISTINGS ON EBAY

Creating a listing on ebay makes lots of people very worried for some reason.

However, I have some good news for you! With our guide below you will be up and flying with listings on ebay in no time. However before we begin on the nitty-gritty of writing an ebay listing we have some golden rules that every eBay seller should follow.

GOLDEN EBAY RULES

1. Be the "customer" at all times.
2. Be truthful and point out flaws.
3. Fill in every box possible. Yes, every box possible!

Now, these rules do seem very simple, however we will explain each one in turn to highlight why we mean each one and what it can mean for your listing and ultimately your sales.

BE THE CUSTOMER

Walk a mile, or at least scroll a mile in your customers shoes.

Always be the customer.

Thinking like a customer, as you are customer yourself.

It may sound a little cliche, but you need to put yourself in the mindset when writing the headline, the description, and taking the photos.

Would this make me click buy?

How would I feel about this listing?

Do these pictures look good enough for the money?

The customer centred questions may sound obvious, however, how many times have you scrolled through eBay and been "hell no" to a listing when you have seen or read something that put you off? I know I have, and you probably have as well.

BE TRUTHFUL & POINT OUT FLAWS

Carrying on with the customer centric approach. All flaws in a product, especially, if the product is second hand or used should be pointed out and highlighted. This should be because you are looking to always be truthful.

Forgetting to mention that knock, nic, or missing manual is only going to end up in the long run leaving you with refunds and complaints and more hassle than a quick sale is worth.

Being truthful is good for business.

FILL IN EVERY BOX

eBay is an old website. However, it is also a very sophisticated website, that overtime has become, 'under the hood' a real piece of work (in a good way).

Feeding this machine, and eBay is a machine, with the correct data in the correct boxes will help you in two very different ways.

Firstly, it will help you appear in more searches , so the chances of getting a purchase will increase.

Secondly, as more boxes are filled in eBay is going to know more about your listing, so eBay will be able to promote it and include it in the right channels and search results.

Essentially, the information you enter into eBay is the fuel that helps the engine run. Work with the engine.

CREATING AN ADVERT OR LISTING

So let's now move onto how to create a great advert on ebay. Now that we have got the golden principles out of the way, we can now move onto how we can create a great listing on ebay.

You can use either your phone or your laptop to create a listing on ebay. The good thing about the eBay app and the eBay desktop site from a listing perspective is its synchronization. This is a time-saver, meaning you can quickly switch between the two easily and swifty.

FIVE STEP LISTING

Please note the steps below are based on using the desktop webpage.

1. To begin listing on ebay, go to My eBay at the top right hand corner.
2. Click on selling in the drop down
3. Click on listings tab once the back-end selling hub opens up.
4. Click on 'Create Listing', the big blue button in the top right corner. This will take you to the eBay listing form.
5. Fill in the eBay listing form once it loads.

The listing form is a very long form that changes depending on the category of listing you undertake. We have outlined how to fill in the form below.

However, when it comes to listing on eBay there is nothing better than practice.

PART FIVE:

GUIDE TO FILLING IN THE EBAY LISTING FORM

HEADLINE

The headline is one of the most important parts of eBay. Along with the photos that you upload, this will be the biggest influence on purchasing decisions you have.

So writing a good headline is important. Indeed vital.

SIX RULES TO WRITING A GOOD HEADLINE

1. Put the most important word first.
2. Only include words that people search for - no one searches for WOW, Brilliant etc.
3. The title does not have to be a sentence, it can be a collection of relevant words.
4. Try if possible to use the entire space for the headline. Every character if possible.
5. Do not use hyphens - slash's / or / explanation marks ! question marks ? or emojis.
6. You double check the headline asking "would I click this headline".

You can if you so wish, use a subheading, however, this does cost extra money, at the time of printing this was £0.12, which might not sound alot, however, it will cut into your profit without much benefit in your early days. Especially at the price eBay charges for its other fees!

If you are still stuck about what to include in the headline of an item, we suggest you open up eBay and search for the item, filter the results by Sold Listings and review the latest sale and get inspiration.

CATEGORY

Next, you move onto the selection that is the category. For clarification, the category is the type of product e.g. books, DVD's, Children's toys, home, car parts etc etc.

Now from here on in, each category of item will have a separate range of boxes to fill in that are different due to the varying nature of each product type. So we will not focus on explaining each section as this would make a very long and very dull book.

However, we will mention what we said before and that it is important to fill in every box possible. As this will help your listing rise to the top of relevant searches on eBay, and help eBay display it on the advertising network, which is huge.

CONDITION

A quick note on condition. When you are being asked to describe the condition, always be truthful and "err" on the side of caution. For you the item maybe "mint" to the collector it might be in average condition.

Now that you have filled in the boxes that relate to the item you will come across the photo section. Miss the photos out for now. Come back to them last.

ITEM DESCRIPTION BOX

Y ou will now come to the item description box.

This is an important "free text" box that will allow you to describe the item, your shipping notes, any issues about the item. To help make this simpler we have included an example below, so that you get the gist of what we are talking about.

Headline - Describe and Name the product.

Outline the Condition of the product - New or Used Good Condition.

Postage - note how it is going to be packed and who the carrier is going to be.

Add a note about your shop.

Add a note about being open to asking you questions.

Example

<u>Pink Felt Hanging Decoration.</u>

<u>Condition is Brand New.</u>

All items packed very securely for post.

Dispatched Royal Mail 2nd Class.

Please take a look at our shop, we have many items being added daily.

Please feel free to get in touch if you have any questions.

****

Do you notice that we have included very little information above and beyond what is needed. Keeping it simple is the most important part of eBay.

You will move onto the next section - Selling Details.

SELLING DETAILS

In this section, we cover the pricing, type of listing, postage details, advertising rate and few other bits and pieces that make up an eBay advert.

We will progress through each part of the advert in order that they appeared at the time of writing.

FORMAT

This is a choice between Auction style (traditional ebay) or Fixed price. Most items now sold on ebay are at the Fixed price methodology. There are pro's and con's to both types of listings.

REASONS TO GO WITH AN "AUCTION"

- You may sell the item for more than you valued it at.
- Auction listings are exciting.
- Auctions allow you to set a reserve price (that you are happy to sell for) whilst giving You the possibility of maximising the price you receive.
- Auction is the best format for selling unique, rare or collectable items that are in high demand.

REASONS TO "FIX PRICE"

- You get to set the price you want to receive.
- Less stress as the listing comes to an end.
- When the item sells the customer has to pay straight away.
- You can fully appreciate your profit margin before you list.
- You are able to send out offers of discounts that you are in control..
- You can change the price on the listing at any time.
- Best format for selling "run-of-the-mill" products.

START DATE

In regards to listing start date, if this is a rare or high value item that you are thinking about listing to gain an absolute maximum price, then by all means, schedule a start date for the item. However, for most items you are not going to need to change this, so just leave this as the default time.

PRICE

As you are most likely to be using a fixed price method for your sales working out the price is important. However, it is pretty simple:

Item price + Postage & Shipping Costs + Packaging Materials + eBay fee's + Desired Profit = Sales Price.

VAT

The next box is the VAT box. As you are casually selling you do not need to worry about VAT at the moment so leave blank.

TICK BOXES

Next there are two tick boxes. The first tick box covers buyers remaining anonymous and the other about charity donations.

If you want to make a donation click on the charity box, otherwise leave both of these blank.

DELIVERY DETAILS

In this section you will have to fill in three policy areas: Payment Policy, Postage Policy & Returns Policy.

What you include in here is up to you and how what you feel comfortable with as a seller.

You will have to think about this and make the best decision for you.

We do have suggestions:

- Demand immediate payment. Stops shenanigans and time wasters.
- The quicker the dispatch time the more likely people are to buy.
- The longer the return policy the more likely people are to buy.

PACKAGE DIMENSIONS

You can fill this section in if you wish, However, we generally leave this blank.

ITEM LOCATION

This will only display your town/village or city. Our suggestion is always be truthful regarding this. Do not put a location like Brighton, Knightsbridge or Scunthorpe to sound cool and hip. It will not affect your sales.

SELL IT FASTER

This is eBays own in-house advertising platform. Now to be fair to eBay, this is the bee's knees. It takes very little effort to promote your sales on eBay.

With our store we are (at the time of writing making 60%+) of our sales via promoted listings.

The great thing about the promoted listing is you can set a price as a percentage of the final sale price. eBay will also give you the cost of the advertising if it sales through promoted listings.

Your listing is now almost ready to go. All you need to do now is add in the photos.

EBAY PHOTOGRAPHY SCHOOL

Great photographs sell items. The secret to great photographs is no secret, it is just all about keeping it simple, making sure that it is in focus and following these simple steps.

15 STEPS FOR PHOTOGRAPHS

1. Clean and prepare the item so it looks its best.
2. Save your current listing.
3. Open the eBay app.
4. Open the draft for the item you are going to photograph.
5. Once the listing has opened at the top of the listing, there will be a blue cross. Click the blue cross.
6. When presented with options click camera.
7. The ebay app will open up a special camera app that will link straight into your listing.
8. You can now take the photos of the item.
9. Once you have taken the photos click done at the top.
10. Giving it a few seconds the photograph will load into the photo screen.
11. You can move the photos around so that

the best photo is the main photo.
12. Tap or click on each photo to open up the photo editor.
13. Once in the editor click on the button that looks like a mountain with dots around it.
14. This tool will remove the background and give your item a professional white background. The tool is not perfect, so it might require some touching up.
15. Once you have done this for each photo click done.

GOLDEN RULES: PHOTOGRAPHY

1. The photo should be honest.
2. Photograph and reference any knock, scrapes or blemishes on the items in the photos and in the description box.
3. You can take upto 12 photographs. The more photos the better.
4. Do not forget to use the background tool to make the listing look professional.
5. Make sure the item is in focus.
6. Ensure that light is not reflecting away.
7. Use a white background to help the background tool do its business.
8. Do not be afraid to crop the image.
9. Position the image in the centre of the image.
10. If in doubt ask yourself, how would a retail store or professional ecommerce company photograph the item.
11. Do not be afraid to check other peoples photos for ideas and inspiration.

GET READY TO LIST YOUR FIRST ITEM

You have now filled in every box, added in some great photographs. You are ready to click the list. However, before you gallop ahead and click that shiny blue button, make sure to click the preview button and have one last look over the listing.

Some people will leave the draft 24 hours before listing, so they can review it with fresh eyes the next day.

Whatever you decide to do, if you have completed the above steps, clicking "list" on your first item is a nerve wracking experience.

I felt the same.

However, the nerves and worry will soon disappear when you get that notification about your first sale.

PART SIX:

HOW TO SHIP YOUR SALES

HOW TO SHIP YOUR SALES

Taking shipping seriously is good customer service.

It is a great advertisement for your eBay store!

So how do you effectively ship?

Firstly you need to have a range of packaging materials and tools to hand.

Sticky tape
Scissors
Boxes
Mailer envelopes
Bubble wrap

Now do not go and splurge on shipping material. Search your house first and you'll be amazed how much of the above already have in your possession.

Also once you have searched your house if you are still looking for the above items e.g. boxes or bubble wrap etc there are some options to get them for free.

- Go to your local supermarket and ask at the front desk, or your local corner shop.
- Ask neighbors and friends or even put up a request on Facebook.
- Saving money on materials before making sales is vital.
- As it's Important to save as much of the sales as you get.

THE SHIPPING PROCESS

So you've got your materials to ship effectively, now it is time to send that parcel. What are the steps you need to take to ship out a product effectively?

Step 1) Open up the ebay app or the desktop website.

Step 2) Click on the selling tab on the app or on the website click on the my ebay drop down and click on selling.

Step 3) On the app click on waiting dispatch, on the website click on order and then awaiting dispatch.

Step 4) Package and parcel each package carefully. Make sure the address is written clearly for the postie to read.

Step 5) Click dispatch.

Step 6) Take your parcel to the post office or post box. You can if you wish choose to purchase postage through eBay.

Our current method is through the Royal Mails Click-and-Drop. However, as you start, we suggest hard writing the address and physically going into the post office to dispatch until you are happy with the process.

TIPS FOR GOOD POSTAGE AND PACKING

Use bubble wrap if you can - Bubble wrap can be a lifesaver when it comes to sending parcels. Wrap the item and sticky tape the item up so that it is protected during the knocks that it will have on its journey.

Recycle boxes - Reusing materials is one of the most important ways to save money, search your local town for sources of cardboard box gold.

Address Label - Write the address label clearly, put a return address on the back and include a copy of the sales details inside the package.

Sticky tape - Be liberal with sticky tape when thinking about how the parcel might get snagged in the delivery process.

Postage - When you head to the post office, get a proof of postage receipt.

Ask yourself - Ask yourself would you like to receive the item, the way you packaged it, if you had brought it on ebay?

Thank you - Include a thank you with each order, it is a nice thing to do.

When it comes to shipping, if you are in doubt, add more bubble wrap!

SHIPPING AND PACKAGING SHOPPING LIST

If you do decide to go out and buy all the packaging and shipping material we have included a shopping list below.

Brown Parcel Tape - **https://amzn.to/3qCVKaE**

Dispatch Boxes - **https://amzn.to/3jR7KTE**

Clear Tape - **https://amzn.to/3rTnckI**

Shipping Envelopes - **https://amzn.to/3jUSmFM**

Tape Dispenser - **https://amzn.to/3jTNvVe**

Scissors - **https://amzn.to/3dk04Im**

Bubble Wrap - **https://amzn.to/3dvxHaj**

PART SEVEN:

HOW TO MANAGE YOUR MONEY ON EBAY

HOW TO MANAGE YOUR MONEY ON EBAY

Y ou have now made your first sale! Brilliant. Well done. It is a great feeling. When the notification hits your phone for the first time.

So now that you have made sales, the money should soon be hitting your account soon.

Either via eBays managed payments or via paypal. Either way you are now going to have to manage your money, if you are going to turn this into a business.

However, if you are going to be using eBay to declutter and give yourself a few extra quid just go ahead and buy something nice for yourself go out for a nice slap-up meal.

However, make sure to keep some behind to pay for any eBay fees.

We are assuming that you have now caught the "eBay" bug and will be looking to continue along your own eBay journey.

So for us to continue along this path and too ensure that you are going to manage your money from here on in.

The first thing we have to understand is the difference between some key concepts.

KEY ACCOUNTING CONCEPTS

Revenue. Profit. Cashflow. Re-Investment. Drawings. Costs of Sale.

These concepts will help you manage your money from the eBay business.

Please do not fall asleep, it is interesting. Honest.

REVENUE/SALES

This is the total income into the business. This is the total of all the sales and income in any given accounting period.

For example, if in March you made 10 sales of £10, your revenue/total sales for March would be £100.

PROFIT

This is all the money left, after you have spent money on product, shipping, packaging materials, ebay fees and banking fees. This is the money you could theoretically withdraw from the business. Essentially Profit is Sales minus costs.

For example, if you made 10 sales of £10 your revenue would be £100.

However, if you paid £2 per item. The profit would be £80.

£10 sale minus £2 =profit per sale of £8 multiplied by 10 = £80.

CASHFLOW

This is the money that comes into and out of your business. This is the money that comes into your bank account and the money that comes out of your bank account. Managing this money can be tough, especially when you first get started.

A positive cash flow in a given period is more money coming into the business than leaves.

For example a positive cashflow.

You make 10 sales of £10 = £100

You spend £50.

The cashflow is £50 positive.

A negative cash flow in a given period more money leaves the business than comes in.

For example of negative cash flow.

You make 5 sales of £10 meaning a £50 revenue.

You spend £60, meaning you have a £10 negative cash flow.

Cash Flow is different from profit because it is judged on the actual money that enters the business and not based on recorded profits or revenue.

CAPITAL EXPENDITURE

This is for an ebay business the money you spend on buying new products to sell or money spent on equipment or marketing.

For example.:

You make £80 profits as per our example above, you decide to buy 10 more £2 items to replace those you sold.

You also decide to invest in a new product line with 10 items @ £3, taking your total investment to £50 with £30 of the £50 being reinvestment.

DRAWINGS

This is the best bit of accounts: The money you withdraw from the business. Also known as MAKING BANK. This is the money that you can safely take out after you have paid all the bills, costs etc.

We recommend being conservative and sensible in the start of your business.

For example:

You make 10 sales of £10 in one week and decide that you take out £1 per sale, this means you have drawn out £10. There will now be £90 left in the business.

COST OF SALES

This the money you have to spend to make a sale. For an ebay business this is generally taken up with the eBay fees. It also covers some things like packaging materials and postage.

Before we continue further into the accounts wormhole I would live to note something. Do not be afraid of the big bad accounts. This part is not as hard as you think if you follow some simple rules to ensure that you manage your eBay money.

To help clarify the above we

GETTING STARTED MANAGING YOUR EBAY INCOME

So let's begin. To manage the money that your eBay business makes, we recommend the following.

Step 1) Open or use a dedicated bank account. Accounts like Monzo, Tide and Starling all are great places to start. Of course please do the appropriate checks before deciding on an account. It needs to be correct for your circumstances.

Step 2) Open a paypal account linked to your email address. Add this is your eBay account.

Step 3) Set up managed payment on ebay to get paid

or MAKE BANK!

Step 4) Have managed payments move the money into your account once per week (this is better for cash management as daily payments can leave you bamboozled.

Step 5) On a weekly basis you now need to manage this money.

WEEKLY MONEY MANAGEMENT

Managing your weekly money from ebay should now be relatively easy as you have a separate account, you have managed payments and you are now making sales.

You are going to have to budget for:

Postage & Packaging.
Re-investments in stock.
Fee's.
Other Business costs.

This is a headache. However, we have put together a great simple way to ensure that you able to manage the money. We call it the 10% method.

Every Week, when you come to check the account. I would do it either on a sunday evening or monday morning. Follow the below process.

Step 1) Check the income since last week.

Step 2) Divide the income by 10 to give yourself 10% of sales - withdraw this money as your commission/profit/drawings. The percentage is of course up to you. We used 10% as a guide.

Step 3) Review the balance. Keep £100 in the account at all times to pay for postage etc.

Step 4) Any balance above £100 is now yours to use to invest into stock be it new or second hand. This is your capital expenditure balance or reinvestment. If you are using an account like Monzo or Starling account, set this aside into a "pot" or "place".

Step 5) Use the account when spending money on postage, packing fees and buying new stock, and withdraw it from the pot after each purchase of reinvestment spend into the main account.

This way you are managing budgets without even having to "think" about managing budgets.

Step 6) Repeat each week at the same time and day. If you are using Monzo, Starling etc, you can even note what each transaction does so at year's end it will be easy to manage your accounts. Many other bank accounts are of course available.

Hopefully, this will make managing your ebay money easy if you decide to move on to selling on an ebay more professionally.

Please note this is not your annual or legal accounts. You may need an accountant for this.

Please do all relevant checks before embarking on any course of action regarding your finances. I am self-taught, so please double check the above with other sources.

NEXT STEPS

So you have now successfully started your ebay ecommerce journey and you now just have to keep repeating the source or purchase product, list, ship, repeat. We hope that you have found this an interesting read and inspires you too to go out and start your own eBay journey.

We have really enjoyed writing this book and we hope that you also enjoy making some eBay sales.

If you would like some inspiration please take a look at our store Firecats UK - **https://www.ebay.co.uk/str/FirecatsUK**

If you would like any help with your ebay store, please feel free to email me at **joe@firecats.co.uk**

FURTHER READING AND RESOURCES

BOOKS ON ACCOUNTING

We hope these books help you, like they helped us.

Accounts Demystified by Anthony Rice - **https://amzn.to/3qrYMP1**

Accounting and Finance For Non-Specialists by Atrill & McLaney - **https://amzn.to/3b5kP7O**

How to Understand Accounts by David Rouse - **https://amzn.to/3beHezo**

BOOKS ON EBAY SELLING & ONLINE BUSINESS

There are so many books about eBay online, that you could probably start your own eBay store selling. We have outlined a few that you might find useful:

eBay.co.uk For Dummies, 3rd Edition by Marsha Collier - https://amzn.to/2LT1BJU

The Easy eBay Business Guide: The story of one person's success and a step-by-step guide to doing it yourself by Cathy Hayes - https://amzn.to/3aoApfC

Make Serious Money on eBay UK, Amazon and Beyond by Dan Wilson - https://amzn.to/3ap6T9D

How to Sell on Ebay for Beginners: Ebay Selling Secrets for Easy Online Sales by Money Maker Publishing - https://amzn.to/2Nau2Uo

ebay: How to Sell on eBay and Make Money for Beginners by Greg K. - https://amzn.to/3s3IHzD

The Four Hour Work Week by Tim Ferris - https://amzn.to/37mzYAG

Decluttering at the speed of life by Thomas Nelson - https://amzn.to/2ZzbAHP

BANK ACCOUNTS AND PAYMENT GATEWAYS

We mentioned a range of banks and payment gateways. Before you embark on a finance choice make sure that you do your own due diligence that is right for your personal situation. The below is for information purposes only.

PAYMENT GATEWAYS FOR EBAY

Paypal - www.paypal.com/uk

BANK ACCOUNTS

Monzo - monzo.com

Starling - starlingbank.com

Tide - www.tide.co/business/current-account

Atom Bank - atombank.co.uk

Monese - monese.com

SHIPPING AND PACKAGING ITEMS

Brown Parcel Tape - https://amzn.to/3qCVKaE

Dispatch Boxes - https://amzn.to/3jR7KTE

Clear Tape - https://amzn.to/3rTnckI

Shipping Envelopes - https://amzn.to/3jUSmFM

Tape Dispenser - https://amzn.to/3jTNvVe

Scissors - https://amzn.to/3dk04Im

Bubble Wrap - https://amzn.to/3dvxHaj

ABOUT THE AUTHOR

Joseph Henry

This is Joseph's third book. Previous titles include Recruitment Hacks & Political Careers.

Joseph livies in Scotland after fleeing the maddess of southern england.

You can contact joseph on Instagram @homeworkinghenry

BOOKS BY THIS AUTHOR

Political Careers

Helping you get a job in British Politics

Recruitment Hacks

Hacks to make you a better Recruiter.

Both books are published on Amazon.